YOUR TERRARIUM

by
Mervin F. Roberts

Published by T.F.H. Publications, Inc., T.F.H. Building, 245 Cornelison Avenue, Jersey City, N. J. 07302. Distributed in the British Empire by T.F.H. Publications (London) Ltd., 13 Nutley Lane, Reigate, Surrey, England. In Canada by Clarke, Irwin & Company Ltd., Clarwin House, 791 St. Clair Avenue West, Toronto 10, Ontario, Canada. Printed in the U.S.A. by the lithograph process by T.F.H. Lithograph Corp., Jersey City, N. J. 07302.

Distributed to the Book Trade in the U.S.A. by Crown Publishers, Inc., 419 Park Avenue South, New York, N. Y. 10016.

Iguana cover photo by
Gerhardt Marcuse.

1963 by T.F.H. Publications, Inc.
Rights reserved throughout the world.

TABLE OF CONTENTS

INTRODUCTION

Your terrarium is what *you* make it. Make it indoor or outdoors. Two locations. Make it desert, woodland, bog, shoreline, or aquatic. Five environments. So then, here are two times five—ten terrariums to suit your inclination and pocketbook. Mostly inclination, since it doesn't take much cash to turn out something really nice.

Strictly speaking, a terrarium is a kind of vivarium, a slice of nature, mostly enclosed in glass, for keeping terrestrial amphibians and reptiles. However, terrarium keepers have a way of extending their interest beyond the terrestrial, through bogs, to semi-aquatics, and even aquatic environments, each with its own special species of reptiles and amphibians—and this book will go with the hobby—all the way. One reason, incidentally, for this extension is that pet keepers have taken advantage of watertight aquariums. Years ago, a terrarium was often a wood-framed screen and glass enclosure. Today nearly all household terrariums will hold water, and most of them are adaptations of aquariums.

So then, to get started for an indoor terrarium, first visualize the space you want to devote to your hobby and then find an aquarium or a ready-made terrarium in your attic or pet shop to fit the space. If you plan to establish one of the wetter environments, you will do well to buy a new aquarium from your pet dealer. It hardly pays to repair a broken window in an older aquarium these days. For one thing, many tanks are virtually impossible to disassemble without heating them—all over—evenly—to soften the cement. Having disassembled one and replaced the broken glass, it is virtually impossible to reassemble it without still more of the cement-softening heat.

A terrarium, then, is an enclosed, concentrated "natural" environment for herptiles, that is, amphibians and reptiles. A bit of desert with cacti and horned toads (really lizards). Or maybe a pond with water lilies and soft-shelled turtles or tadpoles (not both—the turtles will probably enjoy eating the tadpoles). Or possibly you want something in between—wetter than the desert, drier than the pond.

Terrarium keeping is also a problem in ecology, the relationship of living creatures to each other and their physical environment. Most of us already know, as Darwin purported, that to the English spinster goes the credit for the strength of the British Empire. It seems that she keeps the cats that eat the mice that otherwise would eat the bumble bees that pollinate the clover that feeds the beef that gives the strength to the British Tommy. Everything —people, animals, insects, plants—gets into the ecology act. Now, observe the terrarium. Here, too, everything gets into the act; it is life concentrated into 2,000 cubic inches. Not just one frog in a bare bowl, but herptiles in their environment. And that, briefly, is what this book is about.

The regular aquarium tank makes a readily available and highly adapt-able container for terrarium use. Photo courtesy Metal Frame Aquarium Co.

Except for the degrees of dampness—arid to aquatic, and indoor *versus* outdoor—it is hard to write about, hard to tailor the information to fit only one habitat, or only one animal. For example, the temperature-humidity control is mentioned in the bog chapter, because humidity is more critical there, but actually it could also be repeated in the woodland chapter.

Foods and feeding were set apart because they have an across-the-board usefulness to you. The list of common names, scientific names, and habitats was set aside also, because it, too, has an across-the-board usefulness. Use it when you see an especially appealing specimen in a pet shop and wonder whether it will fit into *your* scheme of things.

The first thing you must do to set up a terrarium is to decide what habitat you want to create within the container. It is impossible to establish a desert, for example, and have it thrive alongside a bog. The animals don't go to-gether, and the temperature in the desert terrarium is one of extremes: hot dry days, cold dry nights, and maybe a little dew in the morning. A bog, on the other hand, has relatively constant temperature and high humidity, probably highest when the noonday sun is steaming out the wet mosses and ferns. Therefore, to spell out the arrangement and management of terrar-iums, the next five chapters will cover, separately, the five major classes of home terrariums, in order of increasing wetness, starting with the desert.

DESERT

The desert provides for its creatures a harsh, violent life full of blazing heat, dust, numbing cold, long droughts. The soil is often rich in minerals and needs only water to make it lush. But when rain comes, it comes suddenly, wets the ground, and is gone again for months or maybe even years. Plants and animals need little water; what they do get, they hoard. Amphibians are rare. There are no slimy, soft-bodied salamanders. A few species of dry-skinned toads burrow deep and come out to breed only during the short wet season. They eat at night and early dawn when the dew is on the ground.

The plants, like the gopher tortoise and the lizards, are scaly or horny, thick skinned. They soak up water when it is available and revel in the sunlight, almost as if they knew that they must store up the heat against the cold night.

The terrarium for a desert habitat need not be an aquarium, since it will never have to hold water, but if a person had five or ten dollars in his hand and wanted a container for a desert habitat terrarium, chances are he would end up buying an aquarium for the purpose. Aquariums are clean and easy to keep clean. They can be covered securely to make escape-proof cages.

Horned toads are among the most popular and interesting animals suited to life in the desert terrarium. They must be kept warm. Photo by Louise van der Meid.

The gopher tortoise is well adapted to life in the desert terrarium, although it will also live in a woodland setup. Photo by Robert J. Church.

They offer four or five viewing surfaces. And if, as is often the case, the pet keeper decides later to keep water turtles or pollywogs, he has a versatile enclosure at no added expense.

The desert needs bright light and warmth. Assuming no direct sunlight, a 10-gallon desert habitat should receive the light and heat of a 60- or 75-watt incandescent lamp for about ten hours a day. Fluorescent light is no good at all for this purpose. The hot red rays present in an incandescent tungsten filament are a more appropriate substitute for the desert sun. The lamp should be mounted so that it doesn't touch glass; the direct heat just might crack a window. Incidentally, if you pay four cents for a kilowatt hour of electricity, the bill for heat and light in your little Sahara would be 75 watts times ten hours times 4c per kilowatt hour, or a total of 3c per day. It is even less expensive to light a less dry environment.

So, now, for the desert there is an aquarium and a light. Next, there must be a cover. The cover keeps pets in and enemies out. Incidentally, enemies of household pets include young children, cats, and mice. The cover should be designed with them in mind. If the screen is large enough to admit a fly, supplemental feeding can be automatic—just keep a piece of fresh ripe fruit in a dish, and the flies will buzz in through the screen—very nice for several species of lizards and most toads, too. Specially designed terrarium covers are available, at nominal cost, in pet shops.

WOODLAND

The woodland habitat is intermediate between bog and desert. Toads, red efts, garter snakes, box turtles, Greek tortoises, skinks, fence lizards, and the American chameleon are good specimens to start with here. It is not warm enough, or dry enough, for horned toads. It is too dry for any slimy salamanders or frogs. In fact the red eft will barely manage; he really does best in a bog-woodland or a bog. When you set up a woodland terrarium, think in terms of contained water rather than water touching the land. Contain the water in a soupbowl or a dishpan sunk into the earth, or use just a tiny watering dish and sprinkle the plants every few days to keep up the right humidity.

The woodland terrarium need not be watertight, but to keep in lizards or snakes it must have a tight cover. Snakes have a phenomenal ability to escape by pushing through or enlarging a tiny crack. Remember that they have nothing better to occupy their time.

If you keep turtles in a woodland terrarium, you may want to design the plantings in a hanging garden arrangement. This will keep the vegetation from getting trampled.

If you keep a bog or shoreline turtle in a woodland environment it will live, even if it isn't too happy, so long as you remember that many turtles

Box turtles are hardy, intelligent animals that will delight their owners for many years if they are given proper care; all land turtles do best if kept in large terrariums. Photo by Robert J. Church.

Some toads, such as this Fowler's toad, are suited to life in the wood-land terrarium. Photo courtesy of the American Museum of Natural History.

Lizards provide a diverse array of terrarium animals. This arboreal lizard is suited to life in the woodland terrarium. Photo by Gerhardt Marcuse.

Any terrarium housing snakes should be kept well covered, as snakes are adept at escape. Photo by Mervin F. Roberts.

must eat under water. Another point to keep in mind with a woodland terrarium is that many of the animals suited to it cannot shed their skins without having ample moisture available to them. On the other hand, if you keep a woodland snake wet all the time it will surely sicken, probably from a fungal skin disease. But this is not to say that the woodland must be practically bone dry at all times. Give it what God and nature doth provide—rain (from a watering can once in a while) followed by a bright drying period of sunlight (or the equivalent from a 150-watt incandescent light bulb). The trick here is to avoid cooking your pets with kindness. Provide your animals with a place to retreat to when things get too hot, too dry, too wet or whatever. Watch them, study the signs, and act accordingly. You cannot remake your animal or his natural requirements. You *can* (with help from good books, your own observations, and advice from your pet dealer) meet your moral obligations as an animal keeper by keeping your pets healthy—or by releasing them. How much time must you devote to their care? When the financier J. P. Morgan was asked how much it cost to maintain a yacht, he answered that if one has to ask, one cannot afford to own one. Somewhat the same with pet keeping. A novice who must ask how much care he must devote really isn't ready to take on this sort of project. Well then, back to the woods.

A 10-gallon terrarium can hold two small snakes or two turtles or several toads or a couple of lizards under 12 inches. Don't crowd your terrarium. Crowding is the first step toward disaster from fights, disease, or starvation, because a small animal is afraid to eat while an enemy or a possible enemy is nearby.

BOG

The bog is the damp woodland, the dry shoreline, the land of mosses and ferns and tree frogs. Too moist for the American toad, too dry for the bull-frog, it is just right for non-aquatic newts and salamanders, ribbon snakes, wood turtles, and some skinks. The bog is an ideal slice of mother nature pie for plant lovers—orchids thrive, and so do the hardy philodendrons. Princess pine and sphagnum carpet the stage for many dainty little things which would not last two minutes in a terrarium with green frogs (shoreline) or hognosed snakes (woodland). A glass-covered aquarium is a must; this is to control humidity. The light should be subdued and the temperature moderate, 75° to 85°F. in daytime, and 65° to 70°F. at night. Cooling at night seems to stimulate daytime appetites. The exact temperature is a challenge to the terrarium keeper. One thing for you to find out when you

This hop toad, a candidate for both the woodland and bog terrarium, makes use of his air-filled throat pouch to amplify his call. Photo courtesy of the American Museum of Natural History.

Muhlenberg's turtle, readily identified by the orange blotch on either side of the head, does well in the bog terrarium, provided that the heat and humidity are kept at proper levels. Photo by Robert J. Church.

buy a herptile from a pet shop is: Where did it come from? Africa?—meaningless. Temperate woodland Africa?—now you have something to set your teeth into, something to set a thermostat for.

This is a good place to mention how temperatures can be kept up without excessive light from incandescent lamps. Buy a thermostatically controlled aquarium water heater. The tube containing the heating element should be at least three inches shorter than the depth of the terrarium. The thermostat can be in an adjoining tube or in the same tube. Mount the unit in a jar. Choose the largest jar which will fit conveniently in a rear corner of the terrarium. Fill the jar with water. Cover the opening in the jar with a perforated closure, or at least a mesh to protect your animals from drowning. Start the electricity and adjust the thermostat for the temperature you want. The delightful dividend of this design is that the humidity is also under your control, so long as you remember to keep the jar full of water. All you need do is vary the size and number of the holes in the closure. To get two temperatures—warm day and cool night—a clock timer is also necessary. Clock timers are often attached to radios, but there isn't much known about what sounds soothe a skink.

SHORELINE

The shoreline habitat attracts and then discourages more beginning terrarium keepers than all others combined. The shoreline is attractive because it is the natural breeding place for many interesting animals. It is discouraging to many beginners because they suddenly discover that their setup doesn't resemble the beautiful one they saw at the zoo — not even a little bit. Why? Because they went at it wrong. They didn't know that the shoreline is also the natural breeding place for bad odors, and where snakes develop skin disorders. The shoreline mud soils the tank windows and wets the table tops.

Well then, how did the zoo succeed? Simple. They keep it simple. A shoreline should be about half water, half land. What kind of water? Clear water (if you want to see your swimming and underwater pets). How to keep it clear? Avoid mud. Make the land area from clean washed sand, wood, stone, moss, plants in pots. No soil, clay, or loam. Separate the land from the water with a partition, such as with a sheet of glass or a row of stones. Arrange the aquarium so that the water area can be siphoned thoroughly without disturbing the land.

This red-spotted newt is searching among the grains of aquarium gravel for something to eat. Photo by Dr. Herbert R. Axelrod.

Do *just* this and you automatically eliminate most of the troubles. Now you have a simple environment *you can control*. It is easy to siphon, flush and rinse, and siphon again. This can be done whenever the water gets the least bit cloudy or smelly from animal droppings or uneaten foods. The flush and rinse can be salt (mild antiseptic) or potassium permanganate' ($\frac{1}{4}$ teaspoon in a gallon of water—a strong antiseptic) or just plain water if all you want to clear up is a slight cloudiness which accumulated gradually.

Another arrangement which some people favor is to use a large sunken dish, bowl, or basin in the "earth" of the terrarium. This is easy to siphon and wipe out before refilling. Another advantage is that the land can contain earthy materials such as clay, loam, or topsoil, and still the water can be cleared easily. Another advantage is that this arrangement permits the use of a non-watertight cage, if one is available for less cost than an aquarium of the same size. On the disadvantage side is the loss of visibility through the side of the water area. Inventive people who get wonderful ideas at about this point in the book often end up as great cage builders and become so infatuated with their designs and the sound of their hammers that they sometimes forget the hobby of terrarium keeping that got them started. Very few of us are more gifted than the chap who designed the terrarium or aquarium on your pet dealer's shelf.

Another secret you should learn from the professional zoo keeper is that it is a mistake to overstock. Keep a few small animals in a roomy terrarium and they will live a long time with little or no problems. Crowd the same species or add several more species and all sorts of problems crop up. Name some? Sure!

Pickerel frogs secrete into water a substance which poisons most other frog species. Kills them quickly, effectively.

Two large frogs and two small ones in the same 20-gallon terrarium can get on for years, but add one or two more and all you will retain is the one largest frog. All the others will be eaten. What happens is that in the uncrowded situation each frog stakes out his claim and stays on his own territory. Strictly. He finds his worms and flies and beetles there. He sits still and minds his own business. Crowd the terrarium and what happens is probably something like this: (1) Territorial wars, (2) Shortage of food, (3) Closeness of frogs of great size difference, (4) What starts as a fight ends as a gobble, (5) Frog (large) eats frog (small). Delicious. Habit forming.

Maybe some frog authority will dispute this speculation into frog sociology, but the gobble is quite final.

A study of territorial boundaries is an important one for you to consider not only when you stock your new terrarium but also every time you add an animal. As you watch your pets you will discover that a frog or toad, some salamanders, and many reptiles will pick a certain area and defend it

These green frogs are well matched in size and will live peaceably together; in stocking the terrarium, remember that some big frogs will eat small ones. Photo by Mervin F. Roberts.

against all comers. It is not hard to think like a frog for a little while so, before you add another animal to your collection, think of what a frog might think of. Who is bigger? Who is smaller? Who will eat me? Whom will I eat? Where can I sit? Can I find food? Can I sun myself? Can I get out of the sun if I get too warm? A big old male bullfrog might have other thoughts, too. Think about them also.

Elsewhere in this book there is a section on foods for terrarium animals. You should remember, however, that the wet warmth of the shoreline habitat speeds decay. This is especially true in a crowded terrarium. One or two uneaten mealworms in a sparsely populated woodland environment might easily "go native" and actually establish themselves until a toad or a skink catches them. The same two mealworms in a crowded shoreline tank might raise quite a stink. Probably the most important special consideration for feeding shoreline animals is that anything smaller than a bullfrog is good food for a bullfrog. This includes, but is not limited to, other frogs, small turtles, ducklings, mice, and even crayfish.

AQUATIC

Some herptiles are almost completely aquatic, so much so that some species are kept with fish, but in this book we will disregard the fish and consider only the reptiles and amphibians. There really aren't too many. You can find them in the list of names and habitats at the end of this book. When you consider that snapping turtles devour anything but their same size brethren, and that soft-shelled turtles are equally as nippy, and that hellbenders and sirens and waterdogs and mud snakes will eat about anything they can half swallow, and that watersnakes are often vicious; when you consider all this, the field narrows. Build a small platform for basking of small turtles and metamorphosing pollywogs, and try a few water newts. If the turtles are small enough, the newts and pollywogs might just squeak by. A lot depends on how much you feed them.

Tropical aquatic herptiles require an aquarium water heater, but if you keep only native species in your home, no artificial heat is required. You should provide an incandescent light for "sunbathing," regardless. Here is where the landing perch becomes important.

Snails will eat the green algae from the aquarium windows. Turtles will eat the snails; so also with the pollywogs. But to get a good overall cleanup, nothing beats the specially designed aquarium glass cleaners. Copper salts

The common smooth European newt is an attractive novelty for the aquatic terrarium, but it, like other soft-bodied animals, should not be confined with animals capable of harming it. Photo by Laurence E. Perkins.

This aquatic terrarium provides a gradually inclined landing perch so that the soft-shelled turtles in the tank will have a place to bask. The filter helps keep the water clean, a very important consideration. Photo by Robert J. Church.

inhibit algae, but they are generally also poisonous to your specimens. Stick to the cleaners and play it safe.

If you build up any sort of stonework for an aquatic habitat, you should be careful with the alkalis present in the cement. Use large stones, and avoid calcium-bearing rocks. Use a minimum quantity of portland cement. Don't cement the stones to the tank. Cement the stones to each other: Design the structure so it can be removed when you want to clean or re-arrange the tank. When the cement is permanently set—a minimum of two days—it should be washed and scrubbed with a 10% solution of hydro-chloric acid (also called muriatic acid). Hydrochloric acid (HCl) can be obtained at most hardware or building supply stores. Then rinse your "castle" and set it into the aquarium. Oh yes! Here is a "must never." You must never move a filled aquarium if it is larger than one gallon in capacity. Siphon it down, then move it, then refill it. Treat it tenderly and an aquar-ium will last for years. The author conned his father into building him a 10-gallon aquarium in 1931. It was made of plate glass in a metal frame and cemented with aquarium cement. It was still watertight more than thirty years later.

Another point to bear in mind with aquatic terrariums is that they don't have to be muddy. The bottoms can be bare or spotted with a little gravel. The less you put in, the less you have to siphon around when you clean up. An aquatic terrarium is hard to keep clean at best.

SELECTING HERPTILES and STOCKING A TERRARIUM

For a beginner the problem of what to start with is quite simple. Start with a (1) few, (2) healthy, (3) small, (4) inexpensive, (5) hardy specimens.

Item one: Few. A 5-gallon aquarium is right for three or four turtles 2 inches long (when measured over the curve of the upper shell). A few 3-inch frogs *or* four or five tree frogs *or* small toads would also suffice for such a container. If the 5-gallon aquarium were set up as an aquatic terrarium for spotted newts and aquatic frogs (available from tropical fish dealers), the limit would be about six or seven specimens. If the same terrarium were used for a desert setup it would be limited to three horned toads and possibly one tiny gopher tortoise or Greek tortoise.

For snakes, the lengths of four sides of the terrarium should add up to no less than the sum of the lengths of the snakes in it. A tank 12 x 30 inches has 12 + 12 + 30 + 30, or 84 inches of sides. If *all* you have in it is snakes, you could squeeze in two thirty-inch snakes and one twenty-four inch specimen. Keep the sizes close, or the large ones may eat the little fellows.

The hot dry woodland of the American chameleon (*Anolis*) is often a beginner's first terrarium. The advantage of an American chameleon is that it is arboreal, and can therefore occupy *vertical* space in the terrarium. The disadvantage of keeping *Anolis* is that the males are scrappy and need plenty of room. A well-planted 5-gallon terrarium for *Anolis* should be stocked with no more than four of these lizards, especially if more than one of them is a male.

An assortment of several families permits a little more crowding than is possible with just one. If you have arboreal tree frogs and terrestrial toads and semi-aquatic turtles in a shoreline or shoreline-bog arrangement you have effectively used up all the space without causing undue crowding. Three toads might be the limit for a small terrarium, but the arboreal frogs —since they are off the ground—will not crowd them. The turtles will stay mostly in the wet part, and since they don't compete with toads for food anyway, a turtle or two should not cause an upset. There you have item one. Stock few animals. Try for variety if you are tempted to crowd them.

Item two is "healthy." This is obvious, but beginners ask: how do I recognize a healthy specimen in the pet shop? Answer: you recognize it by its activity, fatness, color, and price.

Even a horned toad is fast on its feet. Be sure yours can run before you buy it. The same goes for a snake, a turtle, a newt, or a frog. If it is sluggish and seems to be laboring to get about, just leave it. Don't feel sorry for it and take it home to cure it or fatten it or whatever. Just get a good healthy

The well developed dewlap (throat flap) of the male American chameleon is used in courtship and to threaten other males. It is generally exhibited only by healthy chameleons. Photo by Mervin F. Roberts.

animal and take it home to enjoy it. When you lift a tiny turtle out of its showcase it should try to run through the air. It might also try to bite. Wonderful! This is the sort of spunk that comes with health.

Your specimens should be complete. Tails should be smoothly tapered, without kinks. "Toenails" should all be present. Count them. Look at the animal's eyes. They should be clear and bright and sparkling. When a snake is about to shed his skin, he will look sort of milky in the eye. This is normal. He is (normally) most irritable then, too. Unless you know what you are doing, it is best to avoid choosing such a snake until after he has shed. Don't help him shed. To do that might well kill him.

Healthy also means free of wounds, skin blemishes, lumps, cysts, mites or lice, and other parasites like, on aquatic specimens, leeches. All these problems can be cleared up with care and medication. Your pet dealer knows how. Let *him*.

Healthy herptiles are fat. Frogs, salamanders, lizards, snakes, and turtles all get fat when they are thriving. Some lizards are positively swollen, especially at the base of the tail, when they are in prime condition. If they look scrawny it may be that they are on a hunger strike, and a hunger strike can be fatal. The next time you buy a 20-foot reticulated python, see if it appears to have just swallowed a small boy. This is a sign that it is *really* eating well.

Item three in the list is "small." This is the place you save money, gain experience, enjoy watching growth. It is pretty hard to determine how old a full-size turtle is, but a small specimen is almost certainly young. The birth plate should be off the turtle's belly, but a turtle need not be much larger than a silver dollar to be brought up to maturity by a beginner, just so long as it is vigorous and scrappy to begin with.

If you do get a small *Anolis* you should take care not to get a large one too, or the larger will hound the smaller until the little fellow dies of exhaustion or starvation or worry.

Another herptile which sometimes gives a terrarium keeper concern is the caiman, sometimes spelled cayman, always called mean. It too should be small when you buy it. A foot overall is plenty big. Except for a snapping turtle, or more caimans, there are few herptiles it can be kept with. This is how it should be judged. If it looks meek it is probably not at the peak of

All too often baby caimans are given poor care, resulting in chill, starvation, weakness, and death. Make sure that the caiman you purchase has been kept warm and given good care. Photo by Mervin F. Roberts.

its health. Choose one which wants to attack its shadow and you will have no trouble raising it to a size at which it could attack you.

After you have started to stock your terrarium, the die is cast. If you begin a bog establishment with a spring peeper one inch long, any snake added must be thinner than a lead pencil, and not too much longer. Also, no other frog in the same terrarium can be much more than half again as large, and so on. If you feel you want to make a showing and the idea of small specimens doesn't appeal, then at least try to assemble a collection without conflicts. Aim for a group in which the individuals will not compete for food or dominions, and where some of the individuals are not the natural food of the others.

The next item is "inexpensive." "Inexpensive" in *this* book does not mean "cheap." It does mean that you would be making a mistake to choose rare exotic forms for a starter. Buy good healthy acclimated stock from a reputable dealer and be prepared to pay a fair price.

What is a fair price? This is a hard question to answer, but look at it from several angles, and you will be a good judge of values. Angle one: a dealer must retail livestock for a good bit more than he paid for it. He needs this margin to compensate him for animals which die and for those that need medicine, and for food and for the extra floor space needed for livestock as compared to drygoods. On top of all this, he must figure his time for feeding, cleaning, and caring for animals. This is more than his cost for dusting off a shelf or two of cages or aquarium heaters.

Angle two: a dealer can buy raw, unacclimated stock from an importer for as little as one third of the regular wholesale price. This is not the kind of specimen you should stock your terrarium with. If you shop only for price, you may force your dealer to do the same, and before you can stop the cycle, the bottom will fall out of the market. First there will be no good stock at any price, and soon the price cutters will even wreck what little is left to them.

Angle three: How much would you pay a boy in your own home town for a local *native* turtle, lizard, snake, or amphibian? Say, for argument's sake, 30 cents. Now assume that an importer would pay a professional collector in the tropics just one sixth of that small price: 5 cents. He loses 50% of his stock while waiting for the boat or airplane to pick it up: 10 cents. He feeds it, cages it, treats it for disease: 15 cents—plus profit: 20 cents. He ships it to a wholesale distributor: 25 cents. The wholesaler must charge somewhat more than twice that to the dealer to cover his losses, food, handling, delivery, customs duties and business expenses. Total now 60 cents. The dealer loses unless he gets at least three times what he paid: $1.80. This is what you should be prepared to pay as an *absolute minimum* for even the smallest, commonest, hardiest, imported specimen in a petshop.

When selecting terrarium inhabitants, consider their temperaments. Even baby snapping turtles like this one display the quick strike-and-bite that gave this turtle its common name. Photo by Robert J. Church.

Obviously, nasty animals must be kept apart; this costs extra. Heavy turtles, large snakes, and the like run up a big freight bill by their weight alone.

So then, pay a fair price for an acclimated healthy specimen of a common inexpensive species and leave the rare, expensive, delicate ones for the experienced herpetologist or the professional zoo keeper.

This leads to the fifth and final point. You should start with hardy varieties, the inexpensive popular species that have literature about them readily available; these are the kind to buy. When you visit your petshop, look at the rack of booklets and use it to guide you in your selection. If your pet dealer doesn't know anything about a particular species, it is probably likely that he really doesn't know anything *nice* about that species. Tiny tree frogs and slimy salamanders are not for the beginner. Glass lizards drop their tails with slight provocation. Soft-shelled turtles get nipped by other turtles. Musk and snapping turtles are smelly (although hardy), so avoid them, too, at least until you are sure you won't get thrown out of the house along with your terrarium when the family figures out where that awful stink is coming from.

Thumb through the illustrated books. Compare the life history of a particular species with its appearance. Soon you will develop a technique or a sixth sense which will separate the dainty ones from the easy keepers. Horsemen do it all the time, so there's no reason why amateur herpetologists can't! Because—let's face it—by the time you set up your second terrarium, you are hooked. You *are* an amateur herpetologist.

CATCHING YOUR OWN SPECIMENS

In surburban areas, frogs and toads are easiest to catch on a wet night under a street light. They usually cross the road under a light, since the insects they eat are attracted to light. They also move about looking for places to breed on wet springtime evenings. The actual catch is fairly simple. A net helps. Have a jar or can ready—frogs are slippery.

During the daytime it is best to look for the larger frogs in or near the water. Some people are willing to try to catch frogs with their hands, but nets make the work easier. Walk quietly around a pond or stream until you see your frog. Catch it quickly. Again, have something in which you can hold your frog; holding it in the net is a good method. Give your frog no chance to escape; he will jump at the slightest provocation. A muslin bag with a drawstring is handy for field collectors.

Toads can be found in a variety of locations: in or near quiet water, fields and meadows, gardens, and in the tall grass alongside a building. Try damp places near a house before going into the field. When you look for toads or frogs always walk slowly, carefully, and quietly. Stone walls are good hideouts for many toads as well as snakes. Have the courtesy to rebuild any stone wall you tear down in your search.

Also, frogs will strike at a rag on a fishline. Don't use a hook. By the time the frog lets go, you should have a net under him. Move quickly and the frog will have no chance to escape.

Look for newts and salamanders under stones in bogs, marshy spots, and slow fresh water brooks. You will probably find efts nearby on rainy days in woodlands and bogs. Look under flat stones, pieces of bark, and fallen trees. The best time for collecting efts is after a rain, when the ground is still wet.

Water turtles can be trapped in a "catch-alive" animal trap in the water. They will take fish bait. Make sure the trap is not all the way under the water or the turtles caught in it will drown.

Woodland turtles are fond of mushrooms. Watch for V-shaped cuts in wild toadstools. This will tell you if a turtle is nearby.

To catch the American chameleon, found from North Carolina to Texas, lay a sheet under a tree or bush that they were seen in during the day. On a cool evening, shake the tree. Chameleons in the tree will fall onto the sheet, where they can easily be caught with a net. Another method is to catch them asleep on leaves in the evening. Shine a flashlight on them and use a net. In looking for chameleons, try trees, bushes, vines, stone walls, and fences.

Native crocodilians are protected by law, although they are bred on "farms" in semi-captivity. Today, crocodilians for the pet trade are almost exclusively spectacled caimans caught by native collectors in South America.

These native collectors, as Mr. Ferdinand A. deWiess told the author, supposedly use an interesting method on the assumption that "crocs" are very intelligent. As the story goes, the "crocs" know they will get stuck if they put their feet in soft tar. Some will sit by the hour on logs adjacent to soft tar where they can stare at the sticky material. What the natives do is to prepare one log and one board. On the board they place soft tar. On the log they place water-proof glue. The caiman sees the soft tar on the board and immediately climbs on the log (glue-covered) to view the tar which they are smart enough to avoid.

Another way that "crocs" can be caught is by fastening two pointed sticks in the form of an "X" and covering it with bait, usually entrails. The whole is then attached to a stout rope and left. When the "croc" arrives it will

A good technique for capturing a harmless snake is to pin it with a broom; this allows you to grasp the snake firmly at the rear of its head, preventing it from biting you. Photo by Mervin F. Roberts.

In picking up a newly captured snake you wish to keep as a pet, try to support its body as much as possible to prevent injury to it. Photo by Mervin F. Roberts.

grasp the bait so tenaciously that it can be drawn up and put into a crate before it will release the wood over which the bait is fastened. This method is not as interesting as the former, but much more effective.

Turtle eggs are usually found near water in sand where there is plenty of warmth. If, in your search for reptiles and amphibians, you should come across some eggs, don't molest them. If you want a young turtle, come back every day to see if they have hatched. When they hatch, and you are nearby, you can pick the "cream" of the crop.

Snakes may be found in a wide variety of locations. Look in the grass (especially near bushes), in fields, in woodlots, and near stone walls. Garter snakes seem to like to get under rusted sheet metal. There are several popular methods for catching snakes: (1) a noose on a stick, (2) a net, (3) a flour sack, (4) a forked stick, (5) a shoe (on your foot), (6) your bare hands. Basically the technique is the same. First make sure the snake is not venomous. Second, grab it anywhere, except by the tail. Then quickly get hold of the neck immediately behind the jaws. The muslin bag should be long enough to tie and stout enough to last all the way home. Don't cook your specimens by holding them in the sunlight or by keeping them in an auto in the summertime.

FOODS FOR TERRARIUM ANIMALS

Let's start with the hard and fast facts and *then* develop a background of *if's, and's,* and *but's.*

Fact No. 1. Snakes are carnivorous. All snakes eat only animal food. This is a hard fact. Of course, Indian snake charmers and Rudyard Kipling tell us that cobras drink cow's milk—out of a dish. With a spoon or a straw? If *you* have a captive cobra you are either a professional animal handler or a fool.

Snakes eat all sorts of whole live organisms from earthworms, slugs, caterpillars, crickets, birds, rodents, and so on, up to and including swine. They can be trained to eat cut strips of fresh fish, beef, and small dead animals. Most zoos feed the larger specimens on freshly killed or fresh frozen rodents—mice and hamsters probably suffice for 90% of the captive snakes in the 3-foot to 8-foot size range. Smaller snakes in captivity should be offered the following:

Earthworms

Slugs, for some watersnakes

Earthworms

Small fish—let them flap about in shallow water—good for watersnakes, garter snakes

Earthworms

Not-too-hairy caterpillars, crickets, grasshoppers for greensnakes and ringnecks

Earthworms

Toads for hognosed snakes

Earthworms

Frogs for all garter snakes and watersnakes.

Now then, just in case you took the hint, what is this earthworm bit? Simple. The earthworm is a whole organism. It provides roughage, fat, protein, and vitamins. It is easy to find, easy to keep, easy to propagate, inexpensive to buy. Also, and this is the clincher, many home terrarium animals actually *like* to eat earthworms.

Earthworm eaters include all the small water and bog turtles and some land turtles, plus young crocodilians and the ground-dwelling lizards. Also most small snakes except for the tree dwellers. Also practically all frogs and toads. Also practically all tailed amphibians: newts, salamanders, and hellbenders. Also the crayfish and fish, which, in turn, are also eaten—these, too, thrive on earthworms.

Earthworms prosper on simple fare. They like cool, moist, light topsoil with plenty of vegetable matter worked into it. A wooden box 2 feet long by 2 feet wide by 6 inches deep can support a colony of garden earthworms which, in turn, could support the animals in a 7-gallon aquarium. Put an inch or two of humus on the bottom and then fill it to within an inch of the top with screened rich garden topsoil. Mix in a pound or so of grass cuttings or fresh cut-up vegetable leaves. Put in a dozen or so of the largest night crawlers you can buy or catch. Don't use dungworms. Some bait dealers sell dungworms for fishing, but many terrarium animals would rather starve to death than eat them. They are easy to recognize. They have a bad odor and a dark color, and they are smaller than garden variety earthworms.

The dozen or so nightcrawlers you start your worm colony with are breeders; they might be all of a couple of years old. Cover the topsoil with damp leaves and a wet burlap sack. Leave the box alone in a cool basement for two weeks and then check on the dampness of the soil. If it starts to dry out, sprinkle the burlap and then cover the burlap with a thick damp layer of newspaper. Don't stir up the soil any more than necessary to see how things are coming. These breeders will soon produce a crop of wrigglers that can be raised to the size your pets can eat conveniently.

If you have a cat, or mice, you had better make a screen cover for the worm box. Mice will eat the worms and the cat will mess in the soil. When the weather is right, you can raise all the worms you want in a garden mulch pile; actually, the worm box is nothing more than an indoor mulch.

Smaller worm-eating pets will do well on white worms (*Enchytraeus*). These can be bought at many pet shops. White worms can also be propagated in much the same way as earthworms, except that they seem to favor milksop, bits of meat, and cooked vegetables rather than garden mulch. White worms are especially good for efts and tiny newts and salamanders. Most new-born turtles and snakes really don't need them, since they can easily start out on baby earthworms.

Another live food which has been proved through years of trial is the mealworm. It is an article of commerce. You can raise them or just buy what you need and keep them alive indefinitely. To keep them or to breed them you start out the same way. Get a few dozen worms (larvae) and put them in a ventilated gallon tin can. Fill it half full with oatmeal, cornmeal, or chicken mash and toss in a carrot or half a potato. The vegetable will provide moisture. Also stir in a few fistfuls of crumbled newspaper. The "worms" will eat the meal and vegetable. They will grow, shed, and grow some more. Average home room temperature seems right for them. When they are mature as "worms" they will rest in weblike nests and transform into inactive pupae. Then after a week or two a second transformation creates a beetle. This animal cannot fly, but it can crawl; this is why you should set up business in the tin can. These beetles are good food for many lizards, frogs, and toads, but really it is a mistake to use them that way. Leave them alone. They will breed. In a month you will have a culture of

Mealworms are a staple item of diet for horned toads in captivity, but soft-bodied insects also should be offered. Photo by Louise van der Meid.

mealworms working for you. Select what you need, but try to avoid stirring up the meal and paper mix. Just charge it up now and then with more meal and vegetable. Occasionally, the meal should be replaced or partially changed, for the accumulation of mealworm droppings after a long period not only gives a false impression of the amount of meal present but also is unhealthy for the mealworms. Too much moisture will cause mould. The mealworm doesn't really need much moisture anyway.

The mealworm has a good reputation, but not as good as it should. Too often American chameleons are fed a steady diet of "hard" mealworms. This is too much roughage. Another problem is that some people feed their mealworms on just bran. This is poor pickings for mealworms and poor mealworms for your pets. Use oatmeal and cornmeal and keep an eye on the culture; the mealworms really eat a lot of the stuff. Then just pick the soft worms for feeding. Pick them right after they shed, and the roughage will be at a minimum. Since they shed often as they grow, you can find soft worms of practically any size: little ones to feed baby toads and tiny skinks or big inch-and-a-quarter "adults" to tempt even a one-pound marine toad or a bullfrog.

Another available live food is the fruit fly (*Drosophila*). Raising fruit flies, however, offers some obvious disadvantages. The culture is yeasty and often smells like brewery mash. The flies sometimes escape and cluster on the fruit bowl. New cultures must be set up every few weeks, and this often causes a kitchen chaos. Well then, who does like fruit flies? Answer: the American chameleon and practically all the other small lizards, most amphibians (small frogs and toads especially), and even turtles such as the red-ear and the painted. Of course fish love them, too.

This little fly is in fact the ordinary fruit fly so often seen in warm places around sweet fruits. What makes it useful to terrarium keepers is that geneticists have established strains with shriveled (vestigial) wings. They can hop, but they cannot fly. They breed true. And often. Cultures are available from biological supply houses. High school biology teachers often have the catalogs of these firms. Some tropical fish dealers also carry them occasionally, but fruit flies don't lend themselves to over-the-counter sales, since the cultures have a relatively short useful life. Once you have a culture of wingless flies you can keep a colony going indefinitely. You need:

(1) Wide-mouthed jars. Baby food jars are fine. Throw away the covers.

(2) Cotton plugs to stuff into the bottle necks. These permit the flies to breathe. Otherwise the carbon dioxide gas generated by the medium will asphyxiate the flies. A single thickness of fabric stretched over the jar top with a rubber band, sometimes used instead of a cotton plug, is hard to manipulate when you want to shake out just a few flies into the terrarium. Trouble comes when you try to keep the rest from crawling over the rim. Also the "drumhead" of cloth doesn't keep the right amount of moisture in the culture.

(3) Culture medium made from cooked cereal sweetened with molasses, salted lightly and dosed with 1/20 of 1% of benzoate of soda (sodium benzoate)—a preservative often used in the preparation of maraschino cherries and other slightly acid preparations. This preparation can be obtained from your pharmacist without a prescription—if you have the guts to tell him what you want it for.

(4) Crumpled paper toweling is the material the flies and their maggots crawl over. The eggs hatch on it.

(5) Yeast: bakers or brewers yeast, soft *or* dry, is the final ingredient. The benzoate of soda inhibits most moulds, but a culture of yeast will develop at just the right rate at a temperature of 70° or 80° F., to make the meat and potatoes come out even.

You commence as follows: Sterilize jars by filling them with boiling water. Then pour the water and cap each bottle with a cotton plug. Let them stand to cool while the cereal is cooking. Prepare it with salt, as you would if it were for your own table. Add $\frac{1}{4}$ cup of brown sugar or molasses per cup of water used to make the cereal. Add the benzoate. A little arithmetic will show you how much to use. One simple method is to put up a 1% solution in water or grain neutral spirits and then add an ounce of the liquid to every 20 ounces of the culture mixture. Stir, pull the cotton plug, and pour about $\frac{1}{2}$ or $\frac{3}{4}$ inch into each bottle. Ram in a handful of crumpled towel with a spoon and then quickly replace the plug. Let the culture medium cool to room temperature. Shake in a pinch of yeast and a dozen or so fruit flies. In about three days you will see tiny "worms," and in two weeks or so the flies will suddenly start busting out all over. A new crop, at least twice as many as the parent culture, will appear every day for about two weeks. To use them, get a mesh cover for the terrarium and then with the cover off, (1) slap the bottle down on your hand to shake the flies down; (2) unplug the bottle; (3) turn the bottle over, above the terrarium, and slap the bottom again; (4) plug the bottle; (5) cover the terrarium.

The culture medium will be stiff enough to hold tight to the jar and it will hold the paper tight to it. If it looks wet or soupy after it has stood overnight you probably made it too thin, or did not cook it enough. The yeast should gas up the mix a little. This is all right. Remember that if you put yeast into the hot mix you will kill it. The same goes for the flies. They do best between 70° and 80° F.

The housefly is also a good terrarium animal food. European glassblowers make traps to catch flies. Your pet dealer may be able to get one for you. A piece of rotten meat will attract them through a coarse mesh and your pets will catch them. Incidentally, the British use fly maggots for pet food. They call them "gentles."

Tropical fish keepers swear by *Daphnia*—a flealike fresh water crustacean. Some aquatic newts will take them. To get started, buy a culture from your local tropical fish dealer. He will tell you the preferred method for breeding them in your climate.

Brine shrimp are also a favorite fish keeper's food. They are often suggested for small aquatic reptiles and amphibians, but they really aren't worth the bother. Too small for most terrarium animals.

Crickets are an excellent food. The Old World chameleon loves them; so do toads and frogs and even some "field" and "woodland" snakes. There are two good varieties. One, the common wild black cricket often found chirping in the house, eats grass rugs. The other variety is called the grey or Australian grey cricket. It is an article of commerce. Bait stores sell them to fishermen. These eat grain and cereal foods: bread, crackers, etc. They must have water and they cannot stand freezing weather. When they are happy, they are noisy. They also eat grass rugs. The best way to handle them is in small quantities. Use them quickly, but remember to feed and water them while you are holding them for use, or they may kill each other.

A chunk of beef, cut to suitable size, is a welcome repast for young caimans. Photo by Mervin F. Roberts.

A fish fillet makes an excellent food for water snakes. Photo by Mervin F. Roberts.

Crayfish and the fish and aquatic insects available from bait dealers are all excellent terrarium animal foods. Killies and minnows are excellent food for crocodiles and their ilk, and are also good for aquatic turtles and water snakes; a mudpuppy or hellbender might just like your local breed of bait fish, too.

Tubifex worms, well known to fish keepers, are denizens of sewage-laden streambeds. The pet dealers who handle tropical fish do the dirty work, and your newts and aquatic frogs and turtles will thrive on these meaty little red worms. You buy a small ball of worms, in water. Keep it cool. Refrigeration and daily water changes or, better yet, cold running water will keep them alive for days. They need not be fed.

To feed your aquatic and semi-aquatic animals, simply pull a few worms from the ball with a toothpick or a tweezer or a fork. If they get into mud before they are eaten, they will probably live out their natural lives uneaten. The best way to prevent this is to drop them over a bare slate bottom in the water area of a terrarium. Be careful in warm weather not to overfeed. The live or eaten worms will not cause trouble, but the uneaten worms that die will foul the water.

One universal substitute for live food is a good quality canned dog food. Many turtles love it. Some lizards will get through the winter on it, and the

A toad can very quickly flip out its sticky tongue to capture a grasshopper or other insect. Photo courtesy of the American Museum of Natural History.

Horned toads, tameable and friendly, rank with American chameleons as the two most popular lizard pets. Photo by Louise van der Meid.

Worms are good food for this red salamander and other tailed amphibians. Photo courtesy of the American Museum of Natural History.

larger tailed amphibians can often be "educated" to eat it. Roll it into small balls or pellets. Half dry, they will hold together long enough to be picked up and eaten.

It is amost impossible to list *all* the fruits and vegetables and mushrooms and raw meats your lizard, snake, turtle, newt, or frog will or will not eat. Suffice it to say you should provide the food clean and fresh. "Clean" means, for instance, that Old World chameleons (arboreal) should not be forced to pick insects off sandy cage bottoms. The sand they pick up on their sticky tongues might well be their undoing. Fresh is a relative term, but iguanas normally eat buds and fruits from living plants. This is what *they* thrive on.

Here are some rules, and some details. For more specific data on a particular terrarium animal you should refer to a book or pamphlet about that animal. Your pet dealer will help you select the most appropriate text. Pet dealers are professional animal feeders.

Terrarium animals will not overeat. Feed a caiman until he looks as if he will burst. Keep this up for four years and you will have a caiman 5 feet long.

Where possible, you should feed animals on whole organisms. The roughage, muscles, and glands rich in vitamins and hormones of a whole mouse or a whole worm are a more natural food for a snake or a snapping turtle than just the muscle tissue of a fish fillet.

Dr. James A. Oliver, former Curator of Reptiles at New York's Bronx Zoo and presently Director of the American Museum of Natural History, believes it is easiest and safest to feed dead, rather than live, mice to snakes. This is because dead mice can be handled more easily and eliminate the very real danger of having the snake bitten on seizing the mouse. Furthermore, a snake that refuses to feed on dead animals is *not*, with rare exceptions, more likely to eat them if they are alive, as concluded by E. G. Boulenger, former Curator of Reptiles at the London Zoo, after years of study with hundreds of snakes. Proper temperature and other environmental considerations are the keys to success. A humanely quick way to kill mice is to dash them to the floor with force.

If your garter snake naturally eats live worms you should naturally try to provide it with just that.

Where possible, train your animals to eat without force feeding. This phase of terrarium keeping is really a matter of animal psychology and beyond the scope of this book. This is, in a way, a part of the challenge that drives us from the "easy" to the "difficult" species. When a spring peeper takes a moth from your fingers or a Muhlenberg's turtle eats a worm from your hand, the satisfaction is deemed to justify the effort.

Some herptiles do go on hunger strikes when they are captured, and others go on strike after a period of captivity. You may need to use force feeding to keep the animal alive, but you should never make a habit of it, or even do it once except as a last resort.

When a healthy herptile is due for a meal but refuses to eat, you have several options:

(1) If it is native, release it.

(2) Wait until it becomes hungrier.

(3) Compare the temperature, humidity, and sunlight in the animal's enclosure against that in its natural habitat, and adjust as necessary. Remember that if a herptile eats or is forced to eat while it is really too cold the digestive process will stall and the food may rot in its stomach.

(4) Try feeding the animal at another hour of the day—or at night.

(5) Try another food.

(6) Tease the specimen to strike at food; this sometimes works for big frogs and some snakes.

(7) As a last resort, force feed. The details of the techniques depend on the animal and your dexterity. Very often, for example, a snake's mouth can be opened with a broom straw, and a frog or a worm can be started down without too much trouble. When turtles absolutely refuse to eat, you might try smearing a little cod liver oil on their faces. This may irritate a turtle sufficiently to cause it to rub some oil into his mouth, thus stimulating his appetite.

Herptiles enjoy eating. When they don't eat, they are overstuffed or too sick to eat, too hot, or—more likely—too cold, or just not hungry for the menu.

The American chameleons, really anole lizards, are called chameleons because they resemble the true Old World chameleon in their ability to change color. Photo by Mervin F. Roberts.

The plant-eating iguanas, although big, are becoming increasingly popular as terrarium pets. Photo by Dr. Herbert R. Axelrod.

OUTDOOR TERRARIUMS

You are limited in choice of specimens by the local climate when you establish an outdoor reptiliary or outdoor terrarium or outdoor what-have-you. On the other hand, your native pets will have a more natural climate and even a better diet than they could ever get inside.

So, if you live in Arizona, keep desert animals outside. Semi-tropical Florida will support its own semi-tropical and most tropical herptiles, too. If there is a frost where you live, your native pets must be given an opportunity to dig in and hibernate for the cold season. Reptiles become sluggish at varying temperatures, depending on their natural habitat, but generally even the most hardy go into a slump if it is colder than 60° F. Some amphibians are reported being active even before all the snows are gone, but this is the exception which emphasizes the rule. Another consideration is drought or extreme dry heat. If your local climate includes long hot dry spells you should provide an artificial water supply or permit the specimens to "dig in" and estivate. This dormancy, or estivation, is the way herptiles protect themselves from drying out in a prolonged drought. It is similar to the long sleep of hibernation, but is based on hot dryness rather than cold.

The provision you must make for cold and drought is by having a damp digging area in the terrarium. When you lay out the space you should dig a pit deeper than the frost line and fill it with peatmoss, leaves, and light loose loam. Don't pack it. Be sure the drainage is good; it will become a death trap if it fills with water. This pit might be 10 or 12 inches deep in North Carolina or Washington and 30 or more inches deep in the Great Lakes region or in the Adirondacks of New York. You can line it with wood slats, screening, or brickwork laid up dry, or you can leave it as a raw excavation, depending on the texture of the soil. One method is to dig a pit larger than a wooden barrel. Then knock both ends out of the barrel and stand it up in the hole. Backfill around it with sand or gravel to aid the drainage, and fill it with leaves, moss, straw, wood bark, and light loam.

One other provision for your pets is, of course, the enclosure: this can be wire screening—be sure you ditch it in deeper than your animals can dig. The cover is not necessary if all you keep are terrestrial and aquatic amphibians and turtles. The snakes and climbing lizards call for covers, and this means carpentry, termite protection, locks, latches, and some tricky construction work.

One shortcut is to bury a large old-fashioned cast iron bathtub in the garden. This will give you a clean wall and a flat surface for the top to rest on. If you use a tub, provide for adequate drainage or you will surely foul the setup and possibly drown your animals.

When making an outdoor terrarium, make sure that it is ditched deep enough to keep its inhabitants from tunneling under the enclosure material. Photo by Mervin F. Roberts.

British and Continental terrarium keepers go in heavily for outdoor arrangements, but Americans haven't done much along these lines. Portland cement concrete enclosures are popular in Europe and work well if considerations of freeze-thaw action are not overlooked.

Like the indoor terrarium, there should be both sunny areas and protection from the sun. There should be drinking water and bathing water. There should be plenty of room. A circular outdoor shoreline or woodland screened enclosure, 6 feet across, gives you a 19-square-foot area. This would be fine for, say, four large turtles and a half dozen frogs. Don't crowd it, or it will get smelly.

The lower half of the box turtle's shell is hinged across the middle, and as a result both the front and rear portions can bend upward to close the shell like a box. Photo by Mervin F. Roberts.

Male slider turtles vibrate the long claws on their front feet against the female's face during courtship. Photo by Mervin F. Roberts.

The true chameleon has many unusual characteristics, one of which is the ability to move each eye independently of the other. Photo by Gerhardt Marcuse.

Outdoor terrariums in public gardens and zoos are sometimes moated and sometimes built up up with straight or incurving smooth concrete walls. If you have a building wall or an inside corner of a building to work to, you can save some construction costs by using these existing structures and hooking onto them. Choose the exposure carefully to be sure that *both* sun *and* shade are available during all the daylight hours. A careful design pays

The vegetation in this completed enclosed outdoor terrarium provides shade for the turtles kept in it. Photo by Mervin F. Roberts.

This native American painted turtle is more tolerant of cold weather than many of the imported tropical species and is thus more suited to life in an outdoor terrarium. Photo by Robert J. Church.

off when you have a collection of herptiles that can be left unattended for a week. This is a great feature, especially when the family takes off for a vacation.

One nice thing about keeping native herptiles outdoors is that you can always release them without harming the specimen or upsetting the natural balance. Just to avoid confusing the serious herpetologists, it would be a good idea to not release the non-native species even if they thrive in your local climate. It is distracting for a scientist to find a Fowler's toad in San Francisco, still more so to find a colony of western painted turtles in the suburbs of Glasgow. These people take their work seriously, and they are wonderfully considerate to the amateur herpetologist when he needs help or advice. Don't muddy *their* waters with imported species.

The true chameleon is generally a slow-moving creature, but it uses its tongue with swift and deadly accuracy to catch its food. A tree dweller, the chameleon uses a peculiar hand-over-hand climbing action in loco-motion. Photo by Gerhardt Marcuse.

This green iguana uses its long toes and claws to gain purchase on the tree on which it lies. Iguanas, like the American chameleon, have throat flaps which they use in bluff tactics and mating activities. Many iguanas become quite tame in captivity. Photo by Dr. Herbert R. Axelrod.

DISEASES

Herptiles are like humans. They are complicated. Many things upset them: parasites, fungal infections, wounds, dietary problems, old age, overheating, chilling. These things are easy to list, but sometimes hard to cure. If a native pet has a problem, release him. He will probably cure himself. Talk to your local veterinarian if your pet is not native, and worth saving.

Fungal infections are hard to cure. Salt water baths, rinses in dilute potassium permanganate, and soaking in "wonder" drug solutions are all worth trying. Terramycin is a popular remedy for many skin problems of reptiles, and it may be effective for amphibians as well.

Some fungal infections on the skin of reptiles respond to a dilute vinegar bath—two ounces of vinegar in a quart of water for a few minutes twice a week might help some cases. Full strength vinegar swabs on the affected area may also help. Vinegar swabs are also good for removing leeches.

There are literally hundreds of skin diseases and a score of treatments; some diseases respond to only one treatment. Since the diseases often appear

The Gila monster is one of the two venomous lizards in the world, and definitely not a good terrarium animal. (The other venomous lizard is the Mexican beaded lizard.) Photo by Peter Jenkner.

Rattlesnakes and other venomous snakes should be kept only by professional animal handlers or herpetologists. Photo by Mervin F. Roberts.

similar, it is often a chore to find the right one. Concentrate your efforts this way:

(1) Clean water—sterilize the container.

(2) Direct sunlight—ultra violet is lost in glass.

(3) Uncrowded cages—crowding spreads infections.

(4) Release injured or diseased animals—eliminate sources of infection.

(5) Keep animals well fed—vigorous animals resist disease.

(6) Finally, use the remedies—as a last resort.

Incidentally, if your newt loses a toe or possibly even a foot, he may grow a new one, with no help from you. Same goes for a tail. Many lizards and snakes will also regenerate a tail, but the new one is never as nice as the original.

A final note on diseases has to do with troubles herptiles *cause*.

(1) Bites—turtle, lizard, siren, hellbender, and non-venomous snake bites are treated as simple wounds. Use conventional antiseptics and dressings.

(2) Bites—venomous bites of the Gila monster and poisonous snakes require first aid consisting of rest, suction, no stimulants *and* immediate attention from a physician. Don't be a stoic or a hero.

In nature, box turtles prefer open woodland, especially near ponds or brooks.

Newts can be fed pieces of meat or fish, or any of the live foods offered for tropical fish at your petshop.

Arboreal lizards should be provided with branches and twigs to climb
and rest on. Photo by Gerhardt Marcuse.

The grotesque mata-mata lacks the sharp jaw edges in which most
carnivorous turtles seize their prey; it captures its food largely by sucking
in a quantity of water, carrying the prey into the mouth. Photo by
Harald Schultz.

The skin secretions of **Dendrobates**, a conspicuously marked tropical American frog, are used by certain Indians as poison for their arrows. Photo courtesy of the American Museum of Natural History.

(3) Scares—this is worse than cruel, it is criminal. Some people don't like herptiles—waving one at them won't help.

(4) Communicable diseases—not likely, except possibly fungal infections from herptile to herptile.

(5) Warts—from toads, not likely. If in doubt, handle them with a net, and be safe rather than sorry. There is no doubt that the big marine toad, *Bufo marinus*, of Latin America, has enough poison in its skin to kill a dog foolish enough to eat it. Many other skin secretions are also irritating; to avoid them, handle unknown specimens with a net.

(6) Frogs poisonous to frogs—the pickerel frog, *Rana palustris*, will kill other species kept with it by skin contact or possibly just by being in the same water!

(7) Frogs poisonous to other creatures—according to G. K. Noble, one of the greatest authorities on amphibians, the secretions of some species of the frog *Dendrobates* are used by the Indians of Colombia as a source of poison for their arrows.

SOME PRACTICAL HINTS
FOR
TERRARIUM HOUSEKEEPING

Keep it simple. Avoid complicated setups that discourage cleaning.

Plan for the time you will tear it down. No terrarium is "balanced." Eventually you will have to dismantle it. Don't glue or cement or plaster anything directly to the walls or bottom.

Use a stout cover. It is amazing how a tiny tree frog can squeeze through a crack you hardly noticed. Snakes, too, are notorious for escapes.

Don't crowd. Many hard-to-keep species do quite nicely until another specimen or two is introduced.

Provide a variety of settings for animals of unknown habitat. Create areas of light and dark, warm and cool, dry and moist. See what they favor, if in doubt.

Experiment with foods. Discover, if you can, the greatest variety your pet likes. This will be good insurance if your supply of mealworms or fruit flies runs out.

A covered terrarium is important not only for keeping the inhabitants in but also for keeping other pets and inquisitive hands out. Photo by Louise van der Meid.

Toads always appear to be deep in meditation, pondering the problems of the world.

Newts may be kept with fish, so long as the fish are too large to be eaten and too small to eat the newts.

Lizards should not be grasped or caught by the tail, for many lizards employ breaking off the tail as an escape mechanism. Photo by Gerhardt Marcuse.

One of the pleasant things about common amphibians, such as the red-spotted newt, is that you can enjoy capturing them yourself. Photo by Dr. Herbert R. Axelrod.

When selecting animals for your terrarium, choose alert, bright-eyed specimens such as this iguana. Photo by Gerhardt Marcuse.

The terrarium animals you select should be active, inquisitive, and ready to defend themselves. Don't buy animals that are listless. Photo by Louise van der Meid.

Many native American reptiles, such as this spotted turtle, are protected by conservation laws that make it illegal to capture and hold some species. Your best source of pet terrarium animals is your local petshop. Photo by Robert J. Church.

Read the literature. There is a wealth of information about herptiles in your petshop, bookstore, or library. Start with the list in this book and then go on with the bibliographies in the recommended list.

Visit the zoo. You will get ideas for displaying your specimens by seeing what the professionals are doing.

Buy healthy specimens. Don't buy or keep a sick animal. Encourage your pet dealer to stock only the highest quality of exotic herptiles. Then be prepared to pay a fair price for them. Chances are that you will also want to catch your own native collection by yourself.

Learn your local laws. It is unlawful to hold certain reptiles captive, or to sell them, in some states. Turtles, especially, are protected by conservation laws that you should know about.

Avoid venomous snakes, vicious lizards, the Gila monster, and the smelly species. There is no sense killing yourself (or irritating your neighbors) with a dangerous or disagreeable specimen. Incidentally, most of the venomous snakes are difficult to keep healthy anyway.

Young diamondback terrapins are sometimes offered for sale, but they require special care. Diamondbacks need an addition of salt to their swimming water in order to avoid fungal diseases that attack the turtle when it is removed from its brackish element. Photo by Mervin F. Roberts.

An advantage of keeping baby aquatic turtles such as these young sliders is that they can stand more crowding than most terrarium inhabitants, provided that their quarters are kept clean. Photo by Dr. Herbert R. Axelrod.

Many people are amazed to learn that certain frogs actually live in trees. This is **Hyla caervela.** Photo by Gerhardt Marcuse.

Frogs are ideally suited to the aquatic terrarium. Photo by Dr. Herbert R. Axelrod.

NAMES AND HABITATS
OF AMPHIBIANS AND REPTILES
OFTEN KEPT IN TERRARIUMS

Common Name	Scientific Name	Habitat*
American Crocodile	*Crocodylus acutus*	S—A
American Alligator	*Alligator mississippiensis*	S—A
Spectacled Caiman	*Caiman sclerops*	S—A
Snapping Turtle	*Chelydra serpentina*	S—A
Common Musk Turtle	*Sternotherus odoratus*	S—A
Common Mud Turtle	*Kinosternon subrubrum subrubrum*	S—B
Spotted Turtle	*Clemmys guttata*	B—W
Muhlenberg's Turtle	*Clemmys muhlenbergi*	B—W
Wood Turtle	*Clemmys insculpta*	B—W
Common Box Turtle	*Terrapene carolina carolina*	B—W
Three-Toed Box Turtle	*Terrapene carolina triunguis*	B—W
Oranate Box Turtle	*Terrapene ornata ornata*	B—W
Greek Tortoise	*Testudo graeca*	W—D
Northern Diamondback Terrapin	*Malaclemys terrapin terrapin*	S—A
Map Turtle	*Graptemys geographica*	S—A
Eastern Painted Turtle	*Chrysemys picta picta*	S—A
Midland Painted Turtle	*Chrysemys picta marginata*	S—A
Southern Painted Turtle	*Chrysemys picta dorsalis*	S—A
Western Painted Turtle	*Chrysemys picta belli*	S—A
Red-Eared Turtle	*Pseudemys scripta elegans*	S—A
Hieroglyphic Turtle	*Pseudemys concinna hieroglyphica*	S—A
Blanding's Turtle	*Emydoidea blandingi*	B
European Terrapin	*Emys orbicularis*	S—A
Gopher Tortoise	*Gopherus polyphemus*	D—W
Smooth Softshell	*Trionyx muticus*	A—S
Green Anole or American Chameleon	*Anolis carolinensis carolinensis*	D—W
Crested Lizard or Desert Iguana	*Dipsosaurus dorsalis*	D
Common Spiny-Tail Iguana	*Ctenosaura hemophila*	D
Banded Spiny-Tail Iguana	*Ctenosaura conspicuosa*	D
Rhinoceros Iguana	*Metopocerus cornutus*	D
Galapagos Land Iguana	*Conolophis subcristatus*	D

*—The first letter is the recommended terrarium habitat—the second letter suggests the tendency of the animal to also live in a wetter or drier environment. D = Desert, W = Woodland, B = Bog, S = Shoreline, A = Aquatic.

Texas Spiny Lizard or		
Rusty Lizard	*Sceloporus olivaceus*	**D—W**
Fence Lizard	*Sceloporus undulatus*	**W—D**
Texas Horned Lizard		
(or Horned Toad)	*Phrynosoma cornutum*	**D**
Mediterranean Gecko	*Hemidactylus turcicus turcicus*	**D—W**
Ground Skink	*Lygosoma laterale*	**W**
Five-Lined Skink	*Eumeces fasciatus*	**W**
Eastern Glass Lizard	*Ophisaurus ventralis*	**W**
Green Lizard or Dalmatian Lizard	*Lacerta viridis*	**W**
Eyed Lizard	*Lacerta ocellata*	**W**
English Grass Snake	*Natrix natrix*	**B—A**
Northern Water Snake	*Natrix sipedon sipedon*	**S—W**
Florida Water Snake	*Natrix sipedon pictiventris*	**S—A**
Dice Snake	*Natrix tessellatus*	**A—S**
Northern Brown Snake or		
DeKay's Snake	*Storeria dekayi dekayi*	**W—B**
Eastern Garter Snake	*Thamnophis sirtalis sirtalis*	**W—B**
Checkered Garter Snake	*Thamnophis marcianus*	**W—B**
Eastern Ribbon Snake	*Thamnophis sauritus sauritus*	**W—B**
Western Ribbon Snake	*Thamnophis sauritus proximus*	**W—B**
Eastern Hognose Snake	*Heterodon platyrhinos*	**W—B**
Western Hognose Snake	*Heterodon nasicus*	**W—B**
Ringneck Snake	*Diadophis punctatus*	**W—B**
Blue Racer	*Coluber constrictor foxi*	**W—B**
Smooth Green Snake	*Opheodrys vernalis*	**W**
Corn Snake	*Elaphe guttata guttata*	**W**
Pine Snake	*Pituophis melanoleucus*	**W—B**
Milksnake	*Lampropeltis doliata*	**W**
Hellbender	*Cryptobranchus alleganlensis*	**A—S**
Mudpuppy	*Necturus maculosus*	**A—S**
Greater Siren	*Siren lacertina*	**A**
Narrow-Striped Dwarf Siren	*Pseudobranchus striatus axanthus*	**A**
Amphiuma or Congo Eel or		
Ditch Eel	*Amphiuma means*	**A**
Mole Salamanders	Genus *Amblystoma*	**B—S**
Red-Spotted Newt	*Diemictylus viridescens*	
	viridescens	**B—S**
Dusky Salamanders	Genus *Desmognathus*	**W—B**
Woodland Salamanders	Genus *Plethodon*	**W—B**
European Salamander	*Salamandra salamandra*	**B—S**

Continued on Page 62

Although there are only about 200 turtle species living today, these ancient reptiles present a varied assortment of forms and colors. This pretty land turtle comes from South America. Photo by Harald Schultz.

Crocodilians demand respect when handled, even while still small. Photo by Mervin F. Roberts.

The true chameleons are bizarrely fascinating creatures. This three-horned, swivel-eyed relict of ages past is an African species sometimes available to American terrarists. Photo by Karl Alexander.

Continued from Page 59

Common Name	Scientific Name	Habitat
Brook Salamanders or Yellow Salamanders	Genus *Eurycea*	B—S
Spadefoot Toads	Genus *Scaphiopus*	W—D
Natterjack Toad	*Bufo calamita*	W—B
Toads or Hop Toads	Genus *Bufo*	W—B
American Toad	*Bufo americanus*	W—B
Southern Toad	*Bufo terrestris*	W—B
Cricket Frogs	Genus *Acris*	B—W
Tree Frogs	Genus *Hyla*	W—B
Spring Peeper	*Hyla crucifer*	B—W
Green Tree Frog	*Hyla cinerea*	W—B
Fire-Bellied Toad	*Bombina bombina*	S—B
Chorus Frogs	Genus *Pseudacris*	S—B
Bullfrog	*Rana catesbeiana*	S—B
European Common Frog	*Rana temporaria*	S—B
Green Frog	*Rana clamitans melanota*	S—B
Northern Leopard Frog	*Rana pipens pipens*	B—W
Southern Leopard Frog	*Rana pipens sphenocephala*	B—W
Pickerel Frog	*Rana palustris*	B—W
Wood Frog	*Rana sylvatica*	W—B
South African Clawed Frog	*Xenopus laevis*	A—S

BIBLIOGRAPHY

SCHMIDT, KARL P., 1953: *A Check List of North American Amphibians and Reptiles,* sixth edition, University of Chicago Press, Chicago, Illinois. This is a list of all the recognized species. It provides the reference to the publication in which the animal was first described and traces the changes in name and corrections to the description with localities and dates. Also the range and the common name. It does *not* provide descriptions—just tells *where* the animal was found, and *where* the description can be found.

DICKERSON, MARY C., 1906: *The Frog Book; North American Frogs and Toads, with a Study of the Habits and Life Histories of Those of the Northeastern States,* Doubleday, Page and Company, New York. This is a classic. It is heavily illustrated with beautiful photographs and sketches, thorough, competently written. Persistent book hunters can still find this treasure in bookshops and auctions. This is *the* popular work.

NOBLE, G. KINGSLEY, 1931: *The Biology of the Amphibia,* McGraw-Hill Book Company, Inc., New York, Reprinted in 1954 by Dover Publications, New York, in a soft cover. Another classic. This scientific and scholarly treatise is written so a layman can understand and enjoy the subject.

DITMARS, RAYMOND L., *Reptiles of North America,* 1949, Doubleday and Co., Garden City, New York. This is a general, non-technical review written by a man who at one time was Curator of Reptiles at New York Zoological Park (Bronx Zoo).

OLIVER, JAMES A., *The Natural History of North American Amphibians and Reptiles,* 1955: D. Van Nostrand Co., Princeton, New Jersey. This is a thorough and competent treatise for anyone interested in herptiles. Like Dr. Ditmars, Dr. Oliver was also, at one time, the Curator of Reptiles at "Bronx Zoo."

CONANT, ROGER, *A Field Guide to Reptiles and Amphibians,* 1958: Houghton Mifflin Company, Boston. This is the companion to the Checklist. It will fit in a coat pocket. It is thoroughly illustrated. The only drawback to this gem is that the color pictures and short descriptions are not located near either maps or the more detailed descriptions. It has a fine hobbyists' bibliography. This book is probably the most popular of the Field Guides. It deserves to be.

ZIM, HERBERT S. and SMITH, HOBART, M., *Reptiles and Amphibians, a Guide to Familiar American Species,* 1956: Golden Press, New York. This heavily illustrated Field Guide is smaller and less detailed than the Conant Field Guide. And it costs less. It has a soft cover and will fit in a trousers pocket.

This narrow-jawed gavial, **Gavialis gangeticus**, is seldom seen in hobbyists' collections, but it makes an unusual addition for the advanced terrarist. Photo by Peter Irtz.

T.F.H. PUBLICATIONS INC., publishers of this book, provide authoritative, practical, well-illustrated literature for a wide variety of terrarium animals. Consult your pet dealer for a list of available titles.